Step 1
Go to **www.openlightbox.com**

Step 2
Enter this unique code
PLGDT7ZT8

Step 3
Explore your interactive eBook!

Your interactive eBook comes with...

AV2 is optimized for use on any device

 Read

 Audio
Listen to the entire book read aloud

 Videos
Watch informative video clips

 Weblinks
Gain additional information for research

 Try This!
Complete activities and hands-on experiments

 Key Words
Study vocabulary, and complete a matching word activity

 Quizzes
Test your knowledge

 Slideshows
View images and captions

 Share
Share titles within your Learning Management System (LMS) or Library Circulation System

 Citation
Create bibliographical references following APA, CMOS, and MLA styles

This title is part of our AV2 digital subscription

1-Year K–2 Subscription
ISBN 978-1-7911-3310-8

Access hundreds of AV2 titles with our digital subscription.
Sign up for a FREE trial at **www.openlightbox.com/trial**

The digital components of this book are guaranteed to stay active for at least five years from the date of publication.

English Bulldog

CONTENTS

2 Interactive eBook Code
4 Sweet and Dependable
6 Medium-Sized Dogs
8 Coat Colors
10 Growing Up
12 Companions
14 Exercise
16 Grooming
18 Food and Attention
20 Staying Healthy
22 Incredible English Bulldogs
24 Sight Words

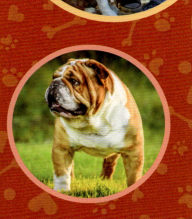

3

My English bulldog is sweet and dependable.

He enjoys spending time with our family.

English bulldogs are medium-sized dogs. They have short, stocky builds and muscular bodies.

Dog Shoulder Heights

French Bulldog
Up to 13 inches
(33 centimeters)

English Bulldog
Up to 15 inches
(38 cm)

American Bulldog
Up to 25 inches
(64 cm)

My English bulldog has darker stripes on lighter fur. This is called a brindle coat. He also has white markings.

English bulldogs can have white, fawn, red, and brindle coats.

English bulldog puppies are small and wrinkly.

They put on muscle and become wider as they grow.

Where in the World

English bulldogs come from the United Kingdom. French bulldogs and American bulldogs were bred from English bulldogs.

English bulldogs make good companions.

They are calm and friendly.

My English bulldog does not need too much exercise.

We take short walks every day.

These walks keep him happy and healthy.

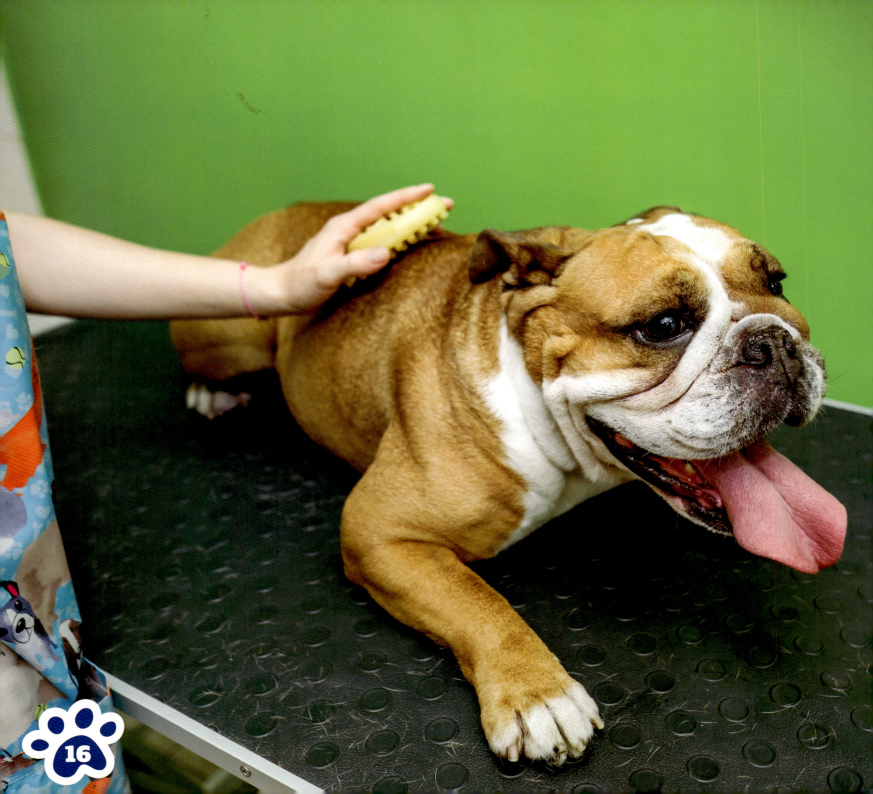

I brush my English bulldog often.

His loose skin has many wrinkles. I clean the folds of his skin to help him stay comfortable.

I feed my English bulldog twice a day.

He likes being near people. My family gives him plenty of attention.

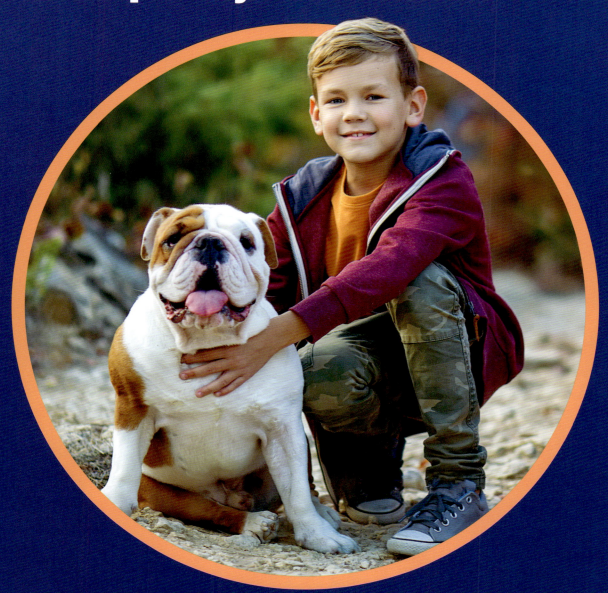

I take my English bulldog to the veterinarian at least once a year.

The veterinarian helps keep my dog healthy.

Dog Breed Popularity in the United States

#6
Dachshund

#7
English Bulldog

#8
Beagle

Incredible English Bulldogs

Most English bulldogs weigh about **40** to **50 pounds** (18 to 23 kilograms).

English bulldogs are known for their **pushed-in noses**.

SIGHT WORDS

Research has shown that as much as 65 percent of all written material published in English is made up of 300 words. These 300 words cannot be taught using pictures or learned by sounding them out. They must be recognized by sight. This book contains 62 common sight words to help young readers improve their reading fluency and comprehension. This book also teaches young readers several important content words, such as proper nouns. These words are paired with pictures to aid in learning and improve understanding.

Page	Sight Words First Appearance
4	and, family, he, is, my, our, time, with
6	are, have, they, to, up
9	a, also, American, can, has, on, this, white
10	small
11	as, come, from, grow, in, put, the, were, where, world
12	good, make
14	day, does, every, much, need, not, take, too, walks, we
15	him, keep, these
17	help, his, I, many, of, often
19	being, gives, likes, near, people
20	at, once, states, year

Page	Content Words First Appearance
4	English bulldog
6	American bulldog, bodies, builds, dogs, French bulldog, heights, shoulder
9	coat, fur, markings, stripes
10	puppies
11	muscle, United Kingdom
12	companions
14	exercise
17	folds, skin, wrinkles
19	attention
20	beagle, breed, dachshund, popularity, United States, veterinarian

Published by Lightbox Learning Inc.
276 5th Avenue, Suite 704 #917
New York, NY 10001
Website: www.openlightbox.com

Copyright ©2026 Lightbox Learning Inc.
All rights reserved. No part of this publication may be reproduced, stored in a retrieval system, or transmitted in any form or by any means, electronic, mechanical, photocopying, recording, or otherwise, without the prior written permission of the publisher.

Library of Congress Control Number: 2024057211

ISBN 979-8-8745-2163-9 (hardcover)
ISBN 979-8-8745-2164-6 (softcover)
ISBN 979-8-8745-2165-3 (static multi-user eBook)
ISBN 979-8-8745-2167-7 (interactive multi-user eBook)

012025
100924

Printed in Guangzhou, China
1 2 3 4 5 6 7 8 9 0   29 28 27 26 25

Project Coordinator: Priyanka Das
Designer: Jean Faye Rodriguez

Every reasonable effort has been made to trace ownership and to obtain permission to reprint copyright material. The publisher would be pleased to have any errors or omissions brought to its attention so that they may be corrected in subsequent printings.

The publisher acknowledges Getty Images and Shutterstock as its primary image suppliers for this title.